Praise for *The Locker Room*

"Occasionally, a book comes along that really impacts you and really makes you think, feel, and want to act differently going forward. This book is a roadmap for how we can progress towards healing, unity, and overcoming the ugliness that is racism. West and Mackey are onto something here, and we should all pay attention because the current game plan isn't working."

—**Rhett Power,**
Forbes **columnist**

"*The Locker Room* comes at a highly contentious time in our country and delivers a powerful and much needed story whose overriding messages of teamwork, unity, and respect for one another are most welcome in the face of increasing social and political divisiveness and a racial reckoning. Set in the inner sanctum melting pot of a football team locker room, former athletes Mackey and West draw on their experiences to present a story that illustrates how teams with players and coaches from diverse backgrounds and ethnicities 'come together around a common goal. They work together, sacrifice for each other, and use their diversity as a strength to make each other better.' The glaring conclusion is that our families and neighborhoods, indeed our country, could benefit from practicing the story's locker room principles and lessons for the betterment of us all. This is a timely, moving, and thought-provoking read."

—**Michael Hurd, historian and author of**
Thursday Night Lights: The Story of Black
High School Football in Texas

THE
LOCKER ROOM

THE
LOCKER
ROOM

THE
LOCKER
ROOM

How Great Teams Heal Hurt, Overcome Adversity, and Build Unity

DAMON WEST

Bestselling Coauthor of *The Coffee Bean*

STEPHEN MACKEY

Player Development Coach

WILEY

Published by John Wiley & Sons, Inc., Hoboken, New Jersey.
Published simultaneously in Canada.

For general information on our other products and services or for technical support, please contact our Customer Care Department within the United States at (800) 762-2974, outside the United States at (317) 572-3993 or fax (317) 572-4002.

Wiley also publishes its books in a variety of electronic formats. Some content that appears in print may not be available in electronic formats. For more information about Wiley products, visit our website at www.wiley.com.

Library of Congress Cataloging-in-Publication Data is Available:

ISBN 9781119897842 (cloth)
ISBN 9781119897866 (ePub)
ISBN 9781119897873 (ePDF)

COVER ART & DESIGN: PAUL McCARTHY

SKY10033313_031722

I dedicate this to my father, Bob West. As a sports writer, you used sports to teach me many valuable life lessons. I still look up to you today, just as I did when I was a kid.

Love,
Damon

I dedicate this to my bride, Teressa. Thank you for your love, support, humility, and grace.

Love,
Stephen

Contents

Preface   *xi*

Prologue The Lifetime Achievement Award   *xv*

1 Eyes on the Prize   1

2 You're Better Than That   11

3 The Locker Room Is Broken   19

4 Growth Takes Place Outside
   of Comfort Zones   25

5 I Believe in You   33

6 Canceling the Cancel Culture   39

7 A Culture of Character   47

8 All In   53

9 The Six Pillars   59

10 In the Zone   67

11 **Vulnerability Is a Strength**   73

12 **Team Meeting**   79

13 **Humility and Grace**   85

14 **I Want the Ball**   93

*Epilogue: A Legacy of Impact: The Lifetime
Achievement Award Acceptance Speech*   *101*

Preface

At the heart of coaching is a deep-rooted commitment to helping people become the best versions of themselves. The role of a coach is to see the potential in people and then do everything within their power to help them get there. As a coach, you're less concerned with the end goal—although *every* coach wants to win!—and more concerned with the progress your athletes make.

Great coaches, as with other great leaders, must be willing to give the best of themselves to set the example for the cultures they wish to build. In that spirit—to give our best to help you become your best—we have created a short story about a team, hurt and divided, which needed the Locker Room to help them heal, unite, and overcome.

Before entering the Locker Room, we would like to offer some insight into a few of the choices made.

We chose the Locker Room as the location of this story because we both have experienced the power of the Locker Room in sports. We are both former athletes (we won't talk about who was the *better* athlete) and have seen the Locker Room break down barriers and transform lives. While the Locker Room is a physical place for athletes, it has its analogues for students in a classroom, executives in a boardroom, workers in any workplace, service men and women in the Armed Forces, and people in their communities. The Locker Room can be made up of 100 people or just two people sitting across from each other.

The Locker Room is anywhere that:

1. People from different backgrounds, with different hurts, hang-ups, and histories come together for a common goal.

2. The standard is the standard, and it isn't lowered because of talent, position, or for short-term gain.

3. Diversity of skill, ability, and personality aren't challenges to overcome, but the very strengths that will allow a team to overcome any challenge.

4. Making a mistake doesn't make you a mistake.

5. Hard days are endured; hard conversations are engaged; hard truths are received; hard consequences grow into encouragement to become your best.

6. Success of the individual is always secondary to the success of the team.

Sports felt an appropriate setting for our story because sports has the power to transcend boundaries; the lessons learned in sports eclipse athletics, helping people become the fullness of who they were created to be.

People from different backgrounds come together in the Locker Room to unite around a common goal. The Locker Room is the setting to engage in difficult conversations about race and discrimination because these are issues that coaches, athletes, leaders, and companies are seeking to address.

The ideas discussed in this story can help anyone begin the conversation toward healing and unity.

We believe that the path to reach our full potential is by people gathering together in their own "Locker Rooms" and having hard, but fruitful conversations, with humility and grace.

The Locker Room is a story about building great culture: your team, organization, or business will be able to immediately apply these principles and grow as a result.

The Locker Room is a story about the importance of great character and a challenge to never let your talent outrun your character. But most of all, *The Locker Room* is a story about the power that each one of us has to make a difference in our own Locker Room, when we choose to give our best for the best of someone else.

Of course, you don't have to be an athlete, or former athlete, for this story to impact you. You just have to be willing to listen.

With humility and grace,

Damon West and Stephen Mackey

Prologue

The Lifetime Achievement Award

The banquet hall at the Berry Center was packed. Coaches, family, media, even the governor had gathered from across the state for the annual Hall of Honor Banquet. Jokingly called "The Ball Coaches' Ball," this was where the best of the best received the ultimate accolades each year. The highest honor, presented at the end, was the Award for Lifetime Achievement.

The winner this year was James Edward Smith.

Coach Smith, known to former players, fellow coaches, reporters, colleagues, and even his own wife as "Coach Smitty," was an exceptional coach. For over 35 years he had served as the head coach of the Tigers of Northwest High School, one of the most successful football teams in the history of the state. It was a surprise to no one that Coach Smitty won this award. Aside from being one of the winningest coaches in the history of the state, his achievement was indeed for his lifetime as a coach: he had just retired after coaching his final season.

Tonight would be Coach Smitty's swan song.

Coach Smitty was a coach who had created a culture of success from his staff and his players. More than three decades earlier, he had written his Six Pillars core values for his team, but when those players graduated, they took the Pillars into other walks of life. Soon, Coach Smitty's tenets were studied by coaching staffs of every sport, at every level. Corporate CEOs would even travel to his annual coaching clinic at Northwest High School to learn from him and see if some of his "magic" would rub off on them.

But it was not magic or alchemy that made him one of the winningest coaches in history. It was his authentic vulnerability. "Authentic vulnerability," he would tell anyone who would listen, "is a strength. By letting your guard down and exposing yourself—with all of your flaws—you can then become that servant leader whom others will want to follow."

Over his storied career, Coach Smitty also endured controversy, especially when it came to his faith. To him, it was worth the flak to instill spiritual principles in the hearts and minds of the boys he would have for four years. Those principles helped ease their transition into becoming men, leaders in their own right. He would say to his assistant coaches, "Everything we are trying to do as coaches comes down to love. If you're not going to love them, you can't coach them!"

His players loved him and his staff in return, as evidenced by 35 years worth of boxes with Christmas cards received every year from the players, photos of children and grandchildren, handwritten letters, and a steady stream of invitations to weddings and christenings. It was evidenced in his career accomplishments and, tonight, in the Lifetime Achievement Award.

The time had come for Coach Smitty's award. The governor had already spoken for 15 minutes to the silent hall, listing first the championships, but dedicating the bulk of his speech to the lives Coach Smitty changed for the better, including his own. Finally, he boomed, "Ladies and gentlemen, it is my honor to present the Award for Lifetime Achievement to my dear friend, Coach James 'Smitty' Smith."

A loud chorus of applause erupted from the audience. Coach Smitty made his way through the crowd, high-fiving and hugging his friends and peers. Once he was at the podium, everyone settled into their seats to hear this living legend speak. He brought no words on paper and spoke from his heart.

"Governor, thank you for that humbling introduction. You forgot the part about how you tried to convince me to quit coaching to run for office. Politics was never my calling, though. I told you my heart is with a less violent sport," Coach Smitty quipped. "No, sir. I was fortunate to do what I love for more than half my life.

"All I've ever wanted to do in my life is be a coach. But, as every man or woman in coaching knows, you have to find the right partner in life if you want to be a coach *and* have a family. In this regard, I won the lottery with my wife." Coach Smitty locked eyes across the room with his wife. "Elise, thank you for not only supporting my dreams but for also nurturing those dreams. You made me a better man so that I could create better men through sports. I love you."

Coach Smitty paused to wipe the tears from his eyes. "I love football. But too many people think sports is just about scoring points. Sure, scoring points matters—if you don't want to win, why keep score? But there is so much more to sports than points on a board."

Coaches around the room nodded in unison. He continued, "Sports teaches us about life, about being on a team to achieve a common goal. Sports teaches us about being a good teammate, which requires accountability—to yourself and to each other. A team that does not have personal accountability from every coach and player will not win on the field, in the office, in the classroom, or in life.

"In sports, as in life, there are challenges and there is competition; every endeavor requires preparation and sacrifice. I have loved that preparation, and I have even loved that sacrifice. But what I've always loved the most about coaching is the locker room. Not the smell, or the piles of laundry; no one can love that," Coach Smitty laughed with the audience. "No, I love the unity of the locker room. In every locker room you'll find athletes from different backgrounds, diverse stories, all with hurts and hang-ups, hopes and dreams. The Locker Room is a place where all these kids, who are all kinds of different, come together around a common goal. They work together, sacrifice for each other, and use their diversity as a strength to make each other better. They enter the Locker Room as individuals but they leave as a team.

"As I look back on my coaching career, it won't be the records or the state championships that I will remember. I will remember the Locker Room—the place where we built relationships, dreamed dreams, had long conversations, grew, laughed, danced, celebrated, and cried. I will remember how special that place is, and I will forever believe that if more people in this great country got to experience their own Locker Rooms we wouldn't have the problems we have today.

"But America doesn't have a Locker Room—we lack a common goal. We want people to sacrifice for us, but we don't want to sacrifice for anyone else. That's why you see so much division and hate. That's why, when we disagree, we scream at each other instead of talking to each other. It's why, when we get hurt, we go and hurt someone else, just to try and make ourselves feel better. It's why we put people down, instead of helping others up."

Coach Smitty paused, this time for his own emotional control. How to get across to this audience how much he believed in the sanctity of the Locker Room? How to communicate to them that the best of human beings comes out in the vulnerabilities shared in these spaces? How to share with an audience who admires and respects him that this is a lesson he himself had to learn?

Coach Smitty once more surveyed the room, taking a deep breath. He relaxed his hands on the podium, leaned back, and cleared his throat.

"Years ago, I had a Locker Room that was divided, hurt, and angry. What happened in that Locker Room that season changed everything for me. The more I think about that year, the more convinced I am that America needs a Locker Room."

1

Eyes on the Prize

Nine games into the regular season, the Tigers had gone undefeated, under-challenged, and were favored by seemingly everyone to win the state championship. This was their year. Coach Smitty could feel it in his bones. Winning was all he could think about, to the point where he began to isolate himself in his office and work longer hours; he had even taken to sleeping in his office just to get in a few more hours of film study.

It was all anyone in the community would talk to him about.

Until the previous weekend.

Late Friday night, Coach Smitty received a call from the superintendent. Friday night calls from the superintendent were never good. Coach Smitty kissed his wife and took the call in his office, getting comfortable in his chair in case it was going to be worse news than expected.

He was told that Davey, the team's star quarterback and a top-100 prospect, was at a party after the game and made some racially offensive jokes. Of course, someone there caught it on camera, posted it to social media, and it was going viral. Coach Smitty had to wake Elise to boot up her computer and show him the video, since he wasn't on social media. His quarterback didn't appear drunk, Coach Smitty noted to himself. But he made a joke, people off-screen laughed, and that egged him on to make some more jokes, each more tasteless than the last. The video cut out, and Smitty sat back in his chair. While he agreed with the superintendent that it was not a good situation, it was also the last thing he wanted to deal with at that point in the season.

News reporters, recruiters, and people from across the state pounced all over Davey. By Saturday morning, Coach Smitty had dozens of emails and text messages requesting an interview or comment. Normally, Coach Smitty was a very transparent and accessible person, but due to the pressure of the season, and the sensitive nature of the issue, he made the decision to handle everything in-house, by himself.

By Saturday afternoon, Coach Smitty was at Davey's home, having a coach-to-family conversation with Davey and his parents. It was standard for offensive remarks to have a set punishment. Social media may have thrown fuel on the fire, but the underlying violation remained the same. Typically, Coach Smitty would have suspended a player in Davey's situation for poor character, lack of judgment, misrepresenting the program, and breaking the player contract. Before that player could be eligible to play again, he would have to run 200 miles of punishment laps. But Davey was anything but a typical player, and his family was not your typical family. They had money, influence, and were used to having the rules changed for them.

With his tunnel vision, Coach Smitty saw Davey's comments as nothing more than a distraction.

Everyone from the school board to band parents had opinions on how Coach Smitty should handle the situation, and they all thought it their duty to share their solutions. By the time he got to Davey's house, he was exhausted with all of the calls to "cancel" his all-American quarterback for telling inappropriate jokes. He knew it was wrong to make an exception for Davey, but he also thought Davey was the team's best chance at winning. And that's all he could think about.

Davey, to his credit, seemed contrite—although he also spoke of feeling betrayed by the "friend" who had been filming him without his knowledge.

After their conversation, Davey's parents thanked Coach Smith for what they thought was his fair approach to their son's youthful indiscretion. They agreed to take away some privileges at home, revoking his allowance for two months and taking his phone away until things blew over, in exchange for Davey being allowed to continue his senior season. Coach Smitty knew that it wasn't the best way to handle the situation, but in his mind, it was more acceptable than the alternatives.

His eyes were on the prize.

He placated the press with a statement addressing how the situation had been handled and how both Davey and the team looked forward to putting this behind them. He arrived at school on Monday tired but resolute that the next few weeks would decide the season and bring a championship to Northwest.

As Monday's morning practice was wrapping up, Coach Smitty blew his whistle and shouted, "Okay men! Grab a knee."

There was never really a need for Coach Smitty to shout. He was as big as a refrigerator and, even though his playing days as a college linebacker were behind him, he still looked like he could strap up and bring the hammer. If he wanted the players' attention, he only had to look at them. His players didn't fear him; they respected him. But today, things were different.

Monday practice periods were usually exciting days. The players were coming off the weekend, which meant they were coming off of a Friday night victory. However, all practice the players had been at each other's throats. Even though they were in helmets and shorts, they were coming at each other a little harder than normal. The trash talking, too, seemed a little more personal.

Most noticeably, though, the respect for each other and the coaching staff was at an all-time low. Despite all of these abnormalities, Coach Smitty decided he was going to focus on the positives.

"Today was a good day, fellas. But good is not what we're after. We want to be elite! To be elite we are going to have to do the little things better than anyone. I want y'all to get focused and be ready to come back for this afternoon's practice ready to prepare for Friday night. Okay, let's break. . . ."

While he was talking, Coach Smitty looked to his left and saw Marcellus and his twin brother mumbling to each other. The brothers were the undisputed leaders of the defense, with talent, leadership, and the elusive "it factor." Their abilities didn't stop at the field, either. They were as bright in the classroom as they were on the field. In fact, both had committed to the same university in the fall so their parents wouldn't have to split time watching them play.

For anybody to be talking while Coach Smitty was talking was a cardinal sin, but for those two to be talking was another sign that something was not right—another sign Coach Smitty missed.

"I'm sorry, gentlemen. I didn't mean to interrupt your very important conversation," Coach Smitty said sharply. "Do you know something I don't know about our opponent on Friday? Do you want to trade spots, Marcellus? Do you think you can coach better than I can? Please, Marcellus, stand up and tell us all what is so darn important that you need to be talking while the rest of us are trying to get ready for the biggest game of the year!"

If it was uncharacteristic of Marcellus to be talking while a coach was speaking, it was even more out of character for Coach Smitty to jump on a player as he had done. Coach Smitty was rarely excitable. A jittery energy had unsettled the team. Players sat perched, nervous and unsure of where to look.

Marcellus stood up, shifting his helmet back and forth in his hands. He was never one to shy away from leadership or speaking in public, but he had never seen Coach Smitty act like he just had.

"Well, Coach, it's just that we all heard what Davey said last weekend, but we haven't talked about it as a team. And you're out here acting like it's no big deal that he called us. . . ."

"Last weekend!?" Coach Smitty shouted at Marcellus with such force that he stepped forward into the first row of players.

With the escalation in Coach Smitty's tone, Marcellus adjusted his attitude in kind. Anger replaced fear in Marcellus's face and Coach Smitty saw it. Everyone saw it. It was the same intense look Marcellus had when he roamed the secondary, hunting for the player with the football.

"Yeah, coach! Davey's words made it pretty clear how he felt about his Black teammates. And I want to know what *we* are going to do about it."

That "we" landed like a hammer strike, because Marcellus shot a look to the only Black coach on the team, Coach Washington, looking for backup. Coach Washington, however, would not take his eyes off Coach Smitty. *Figures,* Marcellus thought. *He won't even look me in the eye because he's too scared of Coach Smitty to have our back on this.*

Marcellus continued, "I spent all weekend waiting for you to address it, to make a statement for the team, to call us. Not reporters, or parents, but your team.

But that never came. I guess, when you're Davey, the rules don't apply the same as they do for the rest of us."

Davey, tight-lipped, looked aggrieved, ready to defend himself. The situation was escalating quickly. Coach Smitty, boiling over, lit into Marcellus. "For your information, Marcellus, I took care of Davey's situation this weekend. It's finished. Done. Over. Davey apologized to me and is being punished accordingly. I will not have anyone second guessing how I choose to discipline my players."

Marcellus shouted back, "He never apologized to me! He never apologized to us!" His brother stood up, put his hand on Marcellus's chest, and said, "Stop. It's not worth it." Marcellus stared at Coach Smitty for a long moment, then at Coach Washington, and then slammed his helmet into the ground as he took a knee again.

Coach Smitty, red in the face, began pacing as he addressed the team. "Does anyone else want to interrupt our practice to talk about last weekend?"

When no one dared to speak up, Coach Smitty lowered his tone. "Good. Last weekend is over. Now we move on. This week we have an opponent to prepare for who would love for us to be distracted. Get your minds right, men. I want our practice this afternoon to be focused on Friday night."

When he blew the whistle, the team broke from practice. Everyone jogged off the field, into the locker room.

Everyone but Coach Washington.

2

You're Better Than That

Roderick Washington never thought he would be a coach. Growing up poor, with three brothers, a single mother who worked two jobs to make ends meet, and a father he only met once, he was the very definition of an "at-risk" kid. The odds were stacked against him to even graduate high school, much less go to college and get a master's degree. Sometime in early elementary school, he had been misdiagnosed with a learning disorder and, as a result, no one paid much attention to him, or invested much in him. But, one day, when Roderick was a sophomore in high school, the football coach stopped him in the hall and asked him why he didn't play football. Roderick didn't have a good answer, so the coach asked him to meet him in the locker room after school.

Feeling like he didn't have much of a choice, he showed up, and his life was changed forever. His coaches believed in what he could do; they weren't concerned with what he could not do. They taught him new skills, gave him responsibilities, and then expected him to handle those responsibilities.

They treated him like the man he could become, not the boy that he was. He thought they were the most powerful men he had ever met, because they always used their power and position to build him up, not put him down. Playing sports was, without a doubt, the best thing that ever happened to him.

So after watching his best friend use his power and position to put a kid down instead of lift him up, he knew he had to say something. He jogged after Coach Smitty.

"Hey, Smitty! Wait up." Coach Washington called out as his friend was about to go into the field house.

Coach Smitty turned. "Oh, good, Rod! I'm glad you're here. We need to talk about Friday night. I was thinking...."

"You're right, Smitty. We do need to talk," Coach Washington interrupted. "But it's not about Friday night; I'm not here to talk to you as your Offensive Coordinator. We need to talk, friend to friend."

Coach Smitty could tell by Coach Washington's voice and body language that what was to follow would be best talked about in private. The thing Coach Smitty valued so much about Coach Washington was that he was never afraid to call right, "right," and wrong, "wrong." He motioned them toward his office.

Coach Smitty and Coach Washington had first met when Coach Smitty landed a graduate assistant position at a small D3 school. Coach Washington, a few years older, was the receivers coach. They hit it off immediately. At the time, neither one of them was married, so coaching was their life.

One year later, at a Fourth of July party, they made each other a promise: whichever one of them became a head coach, that person would hire the other. In their minds, they were both thinking they were going to make it big in the collegiate ranks, but after volunteering together at a high school youth camp they both fell in love with coaching high school athletes. Not long after that, Coach Smitty got the job at Northwest High School, a program that hadn't had a winning season in 15 years. It wasn't what they had envisioned when they made their pact, but a promise is a promise, and off they went.

Coach Washington was a phenomenal offensive coordinator. More than anything, though, Coach Washington was the best friend a guy could ask for.

As they walked into his office, Coach Smitty paused at a photo of the two of them at the camp that set them on the path to coach high school football. Then he sat on the couch across from his friend, and said, "Okay, Rod. What's up?"

Coach Washington looked Coach Smitty square in the eyes, took a deep breath, and did something that requires a deep commitment to integrity and to one another—he called his best friend out. "Smitty, I told you on Saturday that the situation with Davey needed to be handled in the open! You disagreed with me and chose to handle it privately. Regardless, I had your back and supported you. You'll always get a 100 percent commitment from me. But that stunt you just pulled out there, what you said to Marcellus. How you treated him was. . . ."

Coach Smitty cut his friend off. "How I treated Marcellus? C'mon, Rod, everyone is making too big of a deal out of this Davey situation. It's not like Davey said the 'N-word.'"

"You think because he didn't say that specific word it lessens the severity of this situation?"

The passion in Coach Washington's voice caught Coach Smitty off-guard.

Coach Washington continued, "Smitty, do you remember that time we had to pull the bus over at a sporting goods store on our way to a road game because we forgot to pack our kicking tee?"

Coach Smitty nodded.

"After a few minutes, I came out and told you they didn't have any kicking tees, and you could tell that I was bothered. Why was I bothered?" Coach Washington asked.

After a pause, Coach Smitty answered, "Because a guy in the store said something awful to you."

"That's right. It wasn't the 'N-word,'" Coach Washington reminded him, "but it was still very hurtful. So hurtful that you went inside and gave the guy a piece of your mind."

Humbled, Coach Smitty understood the point his friend was making. "You're so right, Rod. I'm sorry. I didn't mean to come down on Marcellus like that. It's just . . . well. You know, we've got a real shot at winning this thing. And we can't let anything take our minds off of that. It's a once-in-a-lifetime opportunity for these kids to have a shot at the big one."

"Smitty, listen to yourself. A real shot at winning this thing? What are you trying to win here?" Coach Washington shook his head. "Don't you remember why we chose to be here? We didn't come here because we thought we were going to win championships. Hell, before us they had barely won a game in 15 years! We came here to win the hearts of these kids and help them become men. And what you did out there . . . that's not the Smitty I know. And it's definitely not going to win any hearts, or championships."

"It was that bad, was it?" Coach Smitty asked, knowing the answer even as he asked the question.

Coach Washington's shoulders dropped. He whispered, "Smitty, it's was worse than you realize."

"No, no. I see it now. I'll get Marcellus in here and apologize." Coach Smitty stood up and started towards the door.

Coach Washington stopped him. "You don't see it, Smitty. This isn't about *you* feeling the pressure to win or snapping at Marcellus. It's bigger than that. And it's going to ruin more than our season. You can't coach your way out of this."

Coach Washington then put his hand on his best friend's shoulder and said, "Smitty, come with me. I want to show you something."

3

The Locker Room Is Broken

The Locker Room

The team had finished dressing out from practice and were waiting in the locker room for the second-period bell to ring. When the heavy door closed behind Coach Smitty and Coach Washington, no one bothered to look up. Like all locker rooms, there were the usual smells—sweat, dirty laundry, and Axe body spray—but the typical excitement, music, and laughter was nowhere to be found. It was quiet, and it was cold.

Coach Washington murmured, "Tell me what you see, Smitty."

"A locker room. Guys getting ready for class, some towels that didn't make it into the basket. . . ." He paused his observation to shout out to a freshman lineman, "Hey, Williams! Stop acting like a freshman. Towels go in the basket, not next to the basket!"

Turning back to his friend, Coach Smitty said, "Sorry, Coach. Where was I? Um, I see guys getting ready for class, laundry baskets, and equipment. On the walls, I see the 'Six Pillars'":

TOUGH PEOPLE WIN

INTEGRITY OVER EVERYTHING

GROWTH FOLLOWS BELIEF

EXCELLENCE EVERYWHERE

RELENTLESS EFFORT

SERVICE BEFORE SELF

"What's your point, Rod? This is all stuff you'd see in any locker room."

"Yes, Coach. Those things are ordinary. But look again. Look past all those things. Look at where the kids are sitting and who they're sitting with."

It was as if Coach Washington's words had turned on a light in a dark room. For the first time, Coach Smitty saw that the athletes were clumped together in groups. Not by grade or position on the field, but by their race. Black athletes on one side of the locker room, Hispanic athletes down at the other end, several groups of white athletes on another side, and a small group of Asian athletes in the corner. His team, undefeated and marching toward its first state championship in school history, had self-segregated itself.

"Rod, What's going on here?" Coach Smitty stammered.

"Coach Smitty," Coach Washington began, "What you are seeing in your locker room is young men doing what they've been taught to do in the face of racial tension: retreat to their own corners. We no longer have one team. We now have multiple teams, each with allegiance to their own race, and about 60 percent of our locker room thinks you are on Davey's team, not theirs."

Coach Smitty began to replay that morning's practice in his mind. The players were agitated, but he had dismissed it as intensity. That was wrong. The guys weren't competing harder to get ready for Friday night; they were at each other's throats! It was starting to come into focus for him.

Coach Smitty looked to Coach Washington and, in that moment, he felt more than shame. He felt the weight of disappointing those who had trusted him to lead them, and of letting down his athletes, himself, and his best friend.

His shoulders slumped. "Rod, I am so very sorry," he said, "I can't believe that I didn't see this. You told me on Saturday that I needed to talk about the incident with the team, but I ignored you. The pressure. The championship. The fear of what people would say. I messed up. I am so, so, very sorry."

Before Coach Washington could respond, the bell for second period rang and the athletes, segregated by race, began to file out, group by group. Not a single person said a word to Coach Smitty. Neither Marcellus nor Davey would meet his eyes as they passed.

The two coaches stood in the doorway of the locker room for a few minutes. Coach Smitty, equal parts embarrassed, ashamed, angry, and determined, looked to Coach Washington and said, "Coach, I didn't see it before, but I see it now. From the outside looking in, we've got so much going right for us. But one look inside our locker room and it's obvious we aren't right with each other."

"We'll never be right with each other as long as we've got a broken locker room," Coach Washington agreed.

Coach Smitty thought for a second, and said, "Okay, here's what I'm going to do, Rod. I'm going to do what you suggested this weekend and publicly hold Davey accountable. I'll have Davey apologize to the team. That should fix this problem of his stupid comments last Friday night."

Coach Washington slowly shook his head. "Smitty, you can't fix Monday's problems with Saturday's solution. Just by the fact that you called Davey's comments 'stupid' tells me you have missed what the real problem is here or how to fix it."

Coach Smitty, confused, asked his friend to explain what the real problem was.

"Racism, Smitty. Davey's comments were racist and you backing him up is a by-product of racism. The team isn't right with each other because of racism."

4

Growth Takes Place Outside of Comfort Zones

Of all the things Coach Smitty expected to hear his best friend say was wrong with their team, racism was dead-last on his list. There could be no doubt that what Davey had said was wrong, insensitive, and just plain stupid. But racist? No way!

With his own eyes, Coach Smitty saw the way the boys worked together, and how every player—of every race—followed Davey. They were a team.

Coach Smitty exclaimed, "Rod, don't pull that card on me. We go back too far for that nonsense. How can we have a racism problem? I'm the least racist person I know. If I saw racism, I would call it out. There is no room for that on our team. Every player gets a fair shake from me. If you step on the field in our jersey, it's because you've earned it by your merit, hard work, and dedication."

Coach Washington maintained eye contact, but said nothing. Coach Smitty continued passionately, "I couldn't hold a kid back because of his color, Rod. I don't even see their color. All I see is the blue and gold of our jerseys. And on top of all of that, you're my best friend, Rod, and you're Black! How can we, of all teams, have a racism problem?"

Coach Washington knew he needed to think deeply about his response. It saddened him to see his friend so oblivious, but he realized that Coach Smitty's justification about there being no racism problem was the same reason that racism so often flies under the radar. He knew his friend's heart, so he knew what Coach Smitty was trying to say. He also knew that Coach Smitty didn't see how his reasoning demonstrated a lack of understanding about what racism is.

Coach Washington wondered if anyone had ever sat down with Coach Smitty to help him understand racism. Probably not, since it was such an uncomfortable and polarizing topic. This team—his best friend—needed to have this conversation. Right now, right here.

Well, Coach Washington thought to himself. *Growth takes place outside your comfort zone. Time to grow!* Coach Washington prepared to do what he was put on earth to do: coach.

In his head, he prayed a simple prayer: *Give me the words to speak. Help me be slow to anger, and full of grace.* With each request, he thought about what it was he was asking.

Give me the words to speak*.* How often do people get into difficult conversations with their words sharpened and ready to cut another person down? They talk at a person, instead of with a person. They listen not with the intent to understand another person better, but with the intent to win a debate against an opponent. Coach Washington knew that when you let go of your agenda, your weaponized words, and your prejudgments, you have the space to respond with words that will encourage, challenge, and uplift the person you are speaking with. Those were the words he needed to speak to Coach Smitty.

Help me be slow to anger. Coach Washington lost his mother to cancer during his junior year of college, which made him bitter and angry. Before anger could have a negative impact on his future, his coach saved him by teaching him his "anger rights."

1. You have the right to be angry, but you don't have the right to be disrespectful.

2. You have the right to have anger, but your anger doesn't have the right to have you.

3. You have the right to get angry, but it's not right to get there too quickly.

> His coach told him, "Rule number three is the most important." Adding, "If you are always slow to anger, you can check and double check to make sure you are respectful and in control of your anger."

Help me be full of grace. Coach Washington's pastor once told him, "Justice is getting what you deserve, like when a criminal is punished for his or her crimes. They did wrong and they received just punishment. But grace is altogether different. Grace is getting what you do not deserve. Like if you wronged someone, and they repaid your wrongness with love and forgiveness."

The hardest part about giving grace, the pastor taught, was that it always costs the person giving grace more than it costs the person receiving it.

Simple to pray, Coach Washington concluded to himself, *but difficult to live out*. However, Roderick Washington wasn't one to back down from a challenge. His athletes needed him to *speak up*; he needed himself to be *slow to anger*; his best friend needed some *grace*.

"Okay, Smitty, since we're going to have this conversation, let's make sure we're talking about the same thing, because words are important. Answer me this question: How do you define racism?" Coach Washington asked.

"Well, I guess I would say it is when a person of one race looks down on a person of another race," Coach Smitty replied.

"Good. That's a good place to begin," Coach Washington said. "But what would you say if I told you that what you just described is prejudice, not racism?"

"I would say that I had no idea there was a difference. So, if looking down on another race is prejudice, then what does racism mean?" Coach Smitty asked. He was eager to learn, and he was unwilling to let shame at his prior lack of knowledge hold him back from learning from a willing teacher.

"Racism is about the imbalance of power, meaning that one race has more power than another race, and they wield that power to keep their race's power. So, racism can look like prejudice, but with the added element of power. Let's take this situation with Davey. You are the head football coach. Davey is the quarterback. So, both of you are in positions of power, in our locker room and in our community. You are also both white males. Now, had you dealt with this in the open, the team would have seen you holding Davey accountable for his actions, regardless of his status on the team or his race. But because it was handled in private, it looks like his family's status in the community, his position as QB, and the color of his skin got him the 'Boss's Son' treatment. He was protected by the powers that be, and, as his 'jokes' suggested, he could ridicule people color because of his whiteness. Make sense?" Coach Washington asked.

Coach Smitty was taken back by that, and said, humbly, "Rod, I understand your definitions and it makes sense, but, I honestly don't consider myself to be racist."

"Neither do I!" Coach Washington said, quickly. "You're one of the best men I have ever known. But just because you aren't a racist doesn't mean you can't take racist action. Your decision to not address Davey's behavior out in the open is viewed as racist because of his offensive comments and your willingness to sweep it under the rug.

"It does not mean you're a racist or that you even had racist intent. Heck, you didn't understand the definition of racism until two minutes ago. What it does mean is that you have more to learn about this, and more to learn about your players. And that's why we are having this uncomfortable conversation. What kind of best friend would I be if I didn't jump in this with you, to help you learn. Besides, if the roles were reversed, I know you would do the same thing for me."

"You absolutely know I would, Rod," Coach Smitty exclaimed. "I'm grateful for your friendship."

"And I am grateful for yours. You are willing to learn, which takes humility; I am willing to teach, which takes grace. That, my friend, is the path forward."

Coach Smitty smiled. "Thank you for your grace."

After a moment, Coach Washington asked, "Do you know why I don't apply for a head coaching job of my own? Because I believe in you, Smitty. I believe that you are a leader worth following. I want to be on your team, and whatever good I do through coaching, I want to do it with you. Now let's get to work!"

5

I Believe in You

Coach Smitty stood a little taller, and admitted, "I let our team talent outrun our team character. We can't help these kids win on the field or in life when that happens."

Coach Washington agreed.

The locker room was still cold and it still smelled like sweat and dirty socks, but the air felt lighter—like they'd been at the back of a dark cave and were finally moving toward the promise of sunlight. It was the feeling of acknowledging there was a problem and deciding to move toward a solution.

"So, here we are. We have a broken locker room—our kids are hurting, our team is divided, and a wall of adversity as high as Mt. Everest stands between us and our goals. You got any ideas on how to turn this around, Coach Washington?" Coach Smitty tried to keep hope in his voice.

"Do I have any ideas?" Coach Washington repeated his friend's question, grinning. "Come with me."

Coach Washington led Coach Smitty to the whiteboard on the wall of the locker room.

As Coach Washington erased the football plays off the whiteboard, Coach Smitty asked him, "How can you be so kind to me, Rod? I know we have a long history together but, if anything, I would think that would make my words and actions over the last couple of days even more hurtful, make you more resentful."

"Growing up, there was a guy in my town who hated me and made my life hell."

"Because of the color of your skin?"

Coach Washington gave Coach Smitty a long look. "Partially. But, it was also because I was poorer then he was, and put in with the kids with learning disabilities, so I made an easy target with few defenders. But this highlights an important point. If we're going to heal the hurts of this locker room, we can't make any assumptions when talking to our players." Coach Washington let that important lesson sink in for a moment.

"He would call me horrible names. He would bully me, badger me, and go out of his way to get under my skin. I always just tried to ignore him and take the high road. Until one day, I finally snapped. I came home and he was on my front porch, yelling nasty, awful things through the window to my mother. When I heard him yelling those things at my mother, I just . . . I lost control." Coach Washington looked at the ground, as if he saw the moment clear in his mind's eye.

Without looking up, Coach Washington continued. "With every punch I grew more and more angry. But then, this kid started whimpering. Like a puppy. And the rage just left me in a rush. I stood up and backed off. He looked at me like I was the devil himself, and then he took off running.

"I thought that returning hate for hate would make me feel better. That it would give me closure, or a sense of power. But all it really did was leave me empty.

"My mother came out then and she looked at me like I had been the one shouting at her. She was *that* disappointed in me. She said 'An eye for an eye will leave the whole world blind.' She'd been quoting that at me for years. But that was the first time I understood what she meant. I made a promise to myself that I would repay people's hate, hurts, and hang-ups with humility and grace.

"So, no, Smitty, I'm not angry with you and I'm not resentful. Besides, resentment does no good; it destroys you from the inside out. Like drinking poison and hoping the other person dies."

"Thank you for sharing that, Rod. I . . . I never knew that story," Coach Smitty confessed. "You are one special person, Roderick Washington."

"Nah, Smitty. I'm just a ball coach trying to help another ball coach make a difference. You really want to understand this, right?"

"Of course I do. I'm not going to make the same mistake twice." Coach Smitty pounded his fist into his other hand to punctuate his point.

Coach Washington turned to the whiteboard and wrote in all caps.

6

Canceling the Cancel Culture

THREE QUESTIONS WE MUST ASK:

1. WHERE ARE WE?

"Do you remember going on recruiting trips back in the days of D3 coaching?" asked Coach Washington. "We didn't have GPS or smart phones. All we had were stacks and stacks of printouts from MapQuest. Directions from the office to the first high school, and then from that first high school to the next, and . . ."

"And heaven forbid if we took a wrong turn or got the papers out of order!" Coach Smitty exclaimed. One particularly vivid memory caught him, and he chuckled. "Remember that time we missed that exit off HWY 31, and we didn't know it? Forty miles later we looked at the directions and thought we had the right exit! Ended up at that nursing home in Springfield and not a clue how to get to where we were supposed to be!" Coach Smitty finished the story without realizing he had made Coach Washington's point.

"That's exactly what I'm getting at, Smitty. We had perfect directions, but we had no idea where we were, and so those directions were useless. It's the same way for us and our broken locker room. There are a lot of kids who are hurting right now. Some feel betrayed. Some feel embarrassed or humiliated. There are athletes who are angry at what happened, that are upset about how it was handled. I'm willing to bet there are also some kids in there who feel like

Davey is the real victim here. My point is this: if we want to heal the hurts in our locker room, we—as leaders—have to stop and take the time to listen to our kids, let them hear each other, and give them space to articulate their feelings. We have to know where we are. If we don't, Smitty, we will have lost the game before it ever started."

Coach Smitty knew Coach Washington was right. The best way to help his athletes grow was to start by listening to them.

"Rod, you don't think it will turn into a screaming match?" Coach Smitty asked. He envisioned standing in the middle of a locker room full of frustrated teenagers the size of freight trains spitting insults and hate at each other over the wooden benches.

"Not if you go first and lead the way. Smitty, this isn't cable news where people get paid to pick fights and pretend it's reality. This is our locker room. These kids will follow you. You are proving right now that you have what it takes to lead this conversation."

Coach Smitty furrowed his brow. "I am?"

"To have a tough conversation with others, it requires two things: humility and grace. Both sides must have humility, and you have to be willing to give the best of you for the best of someone else, no matter the cost. You are doing just that. It isn't easy to hear, or say for that matter, the things I told you, Smitty. And it will be even harder to do something about them. But you are bringing the best of you to this challenge, for the best of our team. You're practicing authentic vulnerability, and asking genuine questions. You're taking notes. And, most important, you are listening. When you show the team that humility, they will follow you."

"You really think they will?" Asked Coach Smitty. "I blew it pretty bad."

"I know they will. Think back to when we were stuck in Springfield. Do you remember how hard it was for us to stop and ask for help?"

"Boy, do I! We walked into that gas station like two kids who had forgotten their homework," reflected Coach Smitty with a smile.

"And what happened? They helped us. But, before they could help us, we had to let go of our pride and ask the question, 'Where are we?'"

"That's true." Coach Smitty nodded. "I guess that's the nasty thing about pride. When we hold tight to it, it keeps us from getting where we want to be. We can't begin to heal the hurts in our locker room when we hold too tight to our pride."

"Now you're talking," Coach Washington encouraged. "Like we always tell the boys, 'If you're grippin' you're trippin'."

"Can I be honest with you, Rod?" Coach Smitty asked. "When all this hit on Saturday morning, my first thought was how scared I was that Davey was going to get 'canceled.' I knew what he did was wrong, but I couldn't stand the thought of him losing his future because he made a mistake. Honestly, I was also scared of being 'canceled' myself—for saying or doing the wrong thing. The memories came flooding back of so many other white coaches that, no matter what they did or said on the topic of racism, got themselves into hot water or fired. Nothing those men and women said seemed to be the correct thing. The safest thing for me to do, I believed, was to keep my mouth shut and hope the entire situation blew over.

"I guess that fear, and all the other pressures, really clouded my judgment. It caused me to miss the real hurt that Davey's words caused people I really care about."

"Fear always clouds our judgment. Fear is a liar," Coach Washington offered in support of his friend.

"But what I am seeing now, is that by doing what I did, I really just passed the "cancel culture" from Davey onto Marcellus and the team. When I shut Marcellus down today, I did the very thing that I said I hated so much. I canceled his voice, influence, and perspective. You said it takes humility and grace to have a conversation like this. Well, I don't know that I deserve much grace from Marcellus, or from the team." Coach Smitty stared at his shoes for a long moment.

Finally, Coach Washington broke the silence. "Smitty, you know me well enough to know that I hate cancel culture. In fact, I think it's one of the biggest impediments to healing hurts—people are too quick to be the canceling hand of justice, and they are too slow to be agents of grace. That's why it's so important that we, as coaches, lead the way here. When we lead with humility and grace, there is no room for cancel culture. There is only room to coach people up, encourage them, and tell them the truth: just because you make a mistake, it doesn't make you a mistake."

Conversations like these are why the Locker Room is so special, Coach Smitty thought to himself. Two people talking, like humans. Two individuals, treating each other with respect and dignity.

If only more people could experience this, Coach Smitty thought to himself.

7

A Culture of Character

Coach Washington stepped out to get himself a cup of coffee. Coach Smitty digested what he'd heard, taking in all that he was learning, feeling the rush of understanding something better than he did before. He strolled about the locker room, and as he did, his attention turned to the Six Pillars.

THE SIX T.I.G.E.R.S. PILLARS

(T) TOUGH PEOPLE WIN

I will get knocked down in sports and in life, and I will always get back up—grateful, smarter, and stronger because of it.

(I) INTEGRITY OVER EVERYTHING

I will honor my family, my teammates, and myself by always choosing the "harder right over the easier wrong."[1]

(G) GROWTH FOLLOWS BELIEF

I will be better today than I was yesterday because I will always live and compete as an over-believer.

(E) EXCELLENCE EVERYWHERE

I will give the best of me to whatever is in front of me, always.

(R) RELENTLESS EFFORT

I will not be outworked. My effort is the evidence of my commitment to my family, my team, and my goals, and I will not let them down.

---

[1] Adapted from the "Cadet Prayer" from the United States Military Academy.

(S) SERVICE BEFORE SELF

I will actively look for ways to serve my family, my team, and my community, and will always use my talent, my influence, and my strength for the good of others.

At the start of every practice Coach Smitty would blow his whistle and shout, "I'm looking for a tough, integrity-filled, over-believing, excellence-chasing, stubbornly relentless, selfless servant. Who's it gonna be?!"

Then, all the players on the team would shout out, "It's gonna be me!"

"Who's it gonna be?" Coach Smitty would repeat.

"It's gonna be me!" The players would shout.

It wasn't easy at first, though. When Coach Smitty arrived at Northwest High School, he had to sell his vision of what he believed the program and the players could become. "I expect you to be a champion, on the field and off. If you expect it of yourself, too, we will win championships."

Coach Smitty even had posters made up and placed them throughout the locker room. Each one had the school logo, and one of the Six Pillars. But after several months, he felt that the athletes still weren't buying in. They would say the right words, but the right actions didn't follow. After a meeting with his Captains' Council, one young man shared a sobering confession with Coach Smitty.

"Coach, you tell me that I am a leader, but I've never been taught how to lead."

Following that conversation, Coach Smitty started the Northwest Leadership Academy. The Northwest Leadership Academy was held during the first 30 minutes every Monday, and for the first 10 minutes on other weekdays. He dedicated that time to character and leadership development for all athletes. Coach Smitty would show videos, lead discussions, and provide space for athletes to discuss their ideas.

After a few weeks of the Leadership Academy, he held another Captains' Council meeting, and the athletes suggested adding the Six Commitments to the Six Pillars. "For the Six Pillars to be our standard," they said, "we need to define a standard of behavior, and hold each other accountable to it."

That's also when Coach Smitty established a team contract. Each member of the team, as well as the coaching staff, signed a team contract at the beginning of the year, agreeing to live out these commitments on the field, in the classroom, and in the community. Any player or coach could be called to account for their actions based on these six commitments. For Coach Smitty, accountability was about loving people, and helping them become champions.

Coach Smitty would constantly tell the coaches, "For our players to reach their potential as people, we have to create an environment where love is stronger than anything else—because a person will sacrifice more for love than they will for anything else."

He had created a family atmosphere to cultivate that love. And as he stood in that locker room, it wasn't lost on him that the very culture of character he had built had just called *him* to accountability. This realization gave him a jolt of confidence.

As Coach Washington returned with two Styrofoam cups, Coach Smitty said, "In life, no one keeps track of your wins and losses. They will, however, pay attention to those times when you don't get back up after being knocked down. You have to pick yourself up, lean on others, ask for help, and do whatever it takes to stay in the game. Thanks for helping me back up, Rod."

"You know it, Smitty. When you stand in front of those boys, let your guard down, and show them that all this culture and character stuff you've been preaching isn't just a show. When they see that you really mean it—especially when *you* messed up—they will see that you are authentic, and that you are a leader worth following."

With that, Coach Washington turned back to the whiteboard, and wrote another question in all caps.

8

All In

2. WHERE DO WE WANT TO BE?

Before Coach Washington could cap his dry erase marker, Coach Smitty answered the question on the board.

"This is an easy one! It's the same goal we've had since we first got here: build champions and win championships. That's what the Six Pillars and Commitments are all about. Everything, and I mean everything, we do is to help us reach that one goal."

"Exactly!" Coach Washington agreed. "That's our culture. And we both know that culture is a top-down thing; it's a reflection of leadership."

Coach Washington continued, "But what happens when you, as the head coach, have a vision of where we are going—but the team has a different vision? Or worse, multiple different people on the team have multiple different versions of that vision?" Coach Smitty was quick to respond, "We both know that there cannot be more than one vision. Otherwise, it's like the tug-of-war drill we do in the off-season, with the big battle rope."

The tug-of-war was a favorite team-building exercise in the off-season, because it brought out every ounce of effort each side could give. It also taught the valuable lesson that after all of the chaos, effort, sweat, and tears, there could only be one winner. It was a zero-sum game!

"You're reading my playbook," Coach Washington said with a wink. "Now contrast that with the truck pull event at the Lineman Challenge our boys did last summer."

Coach Smitty was known for thinking outside of the box with his team-building exercises. The previous summer, he had bought a massive, old-time army truck that probably hadn't been driven in 50 years. He had it towed to the parking lot behind the practice field and had one long rope tied to its front bumper. Unlike the tug-of-war, which saw the athletes pulling against each other and in different directions, the truck pull required the linemen to work together as a team to pull the truck 100 yards in the same direction.

Coach Smitty immediately saw the point Coach Washington was making. "When a team doesn't agree on where they are going . . ." he said, drifting off.

". . . then the only place they can arrive at is a broken locker room," Coach Washington finished.

The longer the two men talked by the whiteboard, the more Coach Smitty realized what a big deal this was. On Saturday morning, fear and doubt had kept him from doing what was right, and his team had suffered because of his inaction. So many people depended on him to do the right thing.

Today, however, through a difficult locker room conversation with his best friend and offensive coordinator, he was no longer living in fear; instead, he was living in faith. Faith that humility and grace together can both heal, unite, and overcome adversity.

Coach Smitty had been on a roller coaster of emotion over the course of their conversation. He wondered what his friend was feeling. *How many times had Coach Washington, or his players of color, had to give grace to people who did not understand that their experiences in life were different because of the color of their skin?*

He knew that there was no way he could imagine what Coach Washington was thinking or feeling because at no time in his life had he ever experienced anything similar, due to his race.

But, as a human, he could empathize.

"Rod, we've gotten pretty deep today at the whiteboard. Are you okay?" Coach Smitty asked, with concern.

"Yes, yes we have. We've definitely gotten deep," Coach Washington said, taking a deep breath. "But this has been good. After our conversation Saturday, when you decided to handle this privately, I was angry. Besides feeling ignored, I was angry about the potential harm and distraction this would create for our team, our family. Today, however, I feel like we are going to come out of this thing stronger than before. That feels good."

"I'm truly sorry, Rod. No one wants to feel ignored," Coach Smitty said.

"I appreciate you, Smitty, for being humble enough and open enough to actually listen. To be honest, I have friends and family who get so discouraged and frustrated because they feel like they are always having to show grace and teach white people about race. If I had a nickel for every time a Black parent felt like they did not have time to teach a white person about racism, because they were too busy teaching their Black kids how to survive, I'd be able to buy us that indoor facility we've been dreaming about," Coach Washington said with a chuckle.

Coach Smitty responded, "I owe it to these kids, to you, and to myself to live out the Six Pillars. Especially when it's hard. You asked, 'Where do we want to be?' I'll tell you where I want to be: in this locker room, shoulder to shoulder with you, drawing up the winning plays to fix this broken locker room. Call me crazy, but I think going back to the Six Pillars is exactly where our locker room needs to go."

9

The Six Pillars

Coach Smitty looked at the two questions on the whiteboard. He still had much to learn, but he had opened himself up to learning, and committed himself to listening. Now he wanted to see how much he had absorbed. He thought carefully about his words, and said, "We tell our kids all the time: 'Everything you need to know to be successful in the game of life, you can learn through the game of football.' I think it's time we plug in the Six Pillars to deal with our current opponent." He started drawing on the whiteboard, putting on a Six Pillars coaching clinic for the next 10 minutes.

Coach Smitty drew in big, bold letters: **TOUGH PEOPLE WIN**.

"The conversation we're having is one of the toughest conversations a team or organization can have—that's why so many people, including myself, run away from it. So, if we really want to defeat this opponent, there is only one way—we must be tough! We must be tough enough to love one another, tough enough to give grace, tough enough to be humble, and tough enough to listen and learn. We must get tough to unite our locker room."

Next, he drew: **INTEGRITY OVER EVERYTHING**.

"We ask every member of our program to commit to the 'harder right over the easier wrong.'" There are so many different choices our kids have to make in a day—this makes doing the right thing simple. No matter where you are, or what the details of your circumstance, choose integrity over everything. It's a simple choice that can guide us through complex situations. When we all choose the harder right over the easier wrong, we will learn whatever we need to learn, overcome whatever we need to overcome, and do whatever must be done to heal our locker room. When integrity is the highest value we hold, nothing can keep us from what is right."

Coach Smitty continued on the board: **GROWTH FOLLOWS BELIEF**.

"Position determines perspective. Our world revolves around our experiences. Who we are—what we value, our attitudes and beliefs—is shaped by our perspectives. When I received that phone call on Friday, I thought that if I didn't nip it in the bud, this would derail our season. And that's exactly what has happened. I viewed the situation through my own lens and got a distorted view because my perspective is limited by my experiences. But now, you're helping me see things from a different perspective. Diversity of thought breeds belief in our team as a whole. We are stronger together. This will be an incredible growth moment for our team. We must believe that any adversity is an opportunity for growth. When we believe that, we won't run away from it, but will embrace it, and grow together because of it."

Next, Coach Smitty wrote: **EXCELLENCE EVERYWHERE**.

"This is about so much more than how we practice. This is about how we live! That's why accountability is so important. When we love each other enough to hold each other accountable to this standard, we have the chance to demonstrate our love by being excellent everywhere, and by helping others become excellent when they fall short. How many teams, families, and people have amazing mission statements, core values, or beliefs that they forget to live out when things get tough? It's why good teams cease to be winners. They practice excellence in some places. We've got to bring our values everywhere we go—even into this difficult conversation."

Coach Smitty wrote the fifth pillar: **RELENTLESS EFFORT**.

"What drives our effort? Is it an outcome or a result? No! When we talk about effort, and our unwillingness to be outworked, it's for no other reason than our love and commitment to those who matter most to us. The evidence of our commitment and love of something is our effort. It takes no skill or talent to do this. You can be the best athlete or the worst, but—if you choose to—you can give relentless effort; you can prove your commitment by your effort. How much hurt could be healed or avoided if people were just willing to work through difficult challenges for those they claim they love? And how many people ignore problems just because they think they don't know enough or can't make any real change? Relentless effort tells us that we all have a role to play, if we just care enough to care."

Coach Smitty finished by writing the final pillar: **SERVICE BEFORE SELF**.

"Of all the upside-down things we do, the one I get asked about the most is why we have seniors pick up the field after practice, and why we have them do the things that are traditionally 'freshman jobs.' We elevate and celebrate the role of serving others because we want our kids to launch into life believing that you will never lose by helping other people win, and that the way to the top is by lowering yourself to serve more people. It's the secret to life: servant leadership!"

Coach Smitty took a sip of coffee, then asked, "So, what do you think, Rod? Have I lost my mind? Or could this thing really work?"

"Smitty, you're definitely not crazy. I'm a believer in the Six Pillars. I like where you're taking this thing. I really like the idea of using the Six Pillars to tackle issues beyond the game. This is how we help kids build the long shelf-life skill sets that will help them be successful long after they are done playing ball."

Coach Washington turned to the whiteboard to write the third and final question they needed to answer to complete the most important game plan of their careers. But this time, Coach Smitty stepped up next to him and said, "I think I know the next question, Rod. It's the hardest one to answer."

Coach Washington handed Coach Smitty the marker. Coach Smitty wrote the third and final question on the board.

10

In the Zone

3. HOW DO WE GET THERE?

Coach Washington noticed that Coach Smitty was definitely back to his normal self. In fact, Coach Washington thought that his friend was "in the zone," that magical place in sports where you can't miss. For his part, Coach Smitty felt like he was back in the groove, too. It was as if his friend's grace had removed the anxiety and fears of the last few days, and he could focus on seeing the opportunities in adversity.

"The most difficult part of overcoming any adversity is believing that you can," Coach Smitty said to Coach Washington. "How many times do people give up on something before they even get started because they didn't think they could actually do it?"

Coach Washington replied, "Where you focus, you finish. If you start with 'No' you will find all the reasons you can't do something. But if you start with 'Yes,' you will find all the reasons you can."

"Exactly! There are two things I've learned about adversity. First, it's never as bad as I think it is. I'm always capable of way more than I think I am. . . ."

"And, second," Coach Washington finished Coach Smitty's thought, "Overthinking gets in the way of overcoming."

The two men shared that familiar smile that was unique to their years of coaching together. When they started sharing the same thoughts and finishing each other's sentences, they knew they knew the right play was just around the corner.

"Do you remember that speaker we brought in last year, the one who talked about the power being inside you, not in the world around you?" Coach Smitty asked.

"You bet I do. The kids really related to his parable about the carrot, the egg, and the coffee bean. I see where you're going with this," Coach Washington encouraged.

The story of the coffee bean was one that teams— from junior high to pros—used to illustrate the three choices a person has when faced with the adversity of life, represented by a pot of boiling water. You could choose to be like the carrot, which turns soft in the boiling water. This represented people who were beat down or weakened by adversity. You could choose to be like the egg, whose soft liquid inside became hardened by life, making them mean, angry, and negative. The third choice, however, was to be like the coffee bean in the boiling water. The coffee bean changes the water to coffee because the power inside the bean is transformative, positive.

Coach Washington knew his friend was on the right track, but he also knew that there were still major roadblocks in their path to victory. "So what's the next play, Coach? How can we help these kids be coffee beans?"

"We need to have that team meeting you suggested. In this locker room. Today! I need to own my mistakes in front of the team," Coach Smitty said with resolve in his voice.

"Whoever owns a mistake owns the power to make it right," Coach Washington echoed.

"No doubt. I need to apologize to Marcellus, one-on-one first, then I need to apologize to him in front of the team. And I owe the team an apology," Coach Smitty said, matter-of-factly. "I let them down. This has had a huge impact on our team, and so my apology needs to be proportional."

"This is good, Smitty," Coach Washington agreed. "This will be a path to healing."

"And then, like you suggested, we need to let every player have an opportunity to share how they're feeling, how all of this has affected them, and give them space to tell the truth. To be honest, I'm worried about how it's going to go, but I can't see how we can heal hurts, build unity, and overcome adversity if we don't have a chance for everyone to speak what's in their hearts."

"I know this is a tough one, Smitty, and I'm not trying to throw cold water on you, but what about Davey?"

"It's only tough if I ignore the pillar: INTEGRITY OVER EVERYTHING. Davey signed the team contract just like everyone else. His actions did *not* live up to our standards. It's time I do what I should have done from the beginning: hold him accountable for his actions. This is an opportunity for all of our kids to learn one of the most important lessons they will ever learn—no one is above our standards."

"Are you going to suspend him?" Coach Washington asked.

Coach Smitty had been running from this question from the moment his superintendent called him and broke the news.

"To be honest, Rod, I don't know what I'm going to do. The goal is to build each and every one of our kids into great leaders. There's much that can be learned from this—how to give grace and forgive, how to discipline and how to restore, how to listen and learn. The thing about building leaders, though, is that leaders are not mass-produced. They are handcrafted. So, we're going to have to see how the kids respond, and how Davey responds."

After a brief silence, Coach Smitty looked Coach Washington in the eyes and said bluntly, "The locker room will decide Davey's fate."

11

Vulnerability Is a Strength

The final bell for the school day rang and the players began entering the field house for practice. Monday practice was always one of the most important of the week because it set the tempo for the rest of the week.

From his office, Coach Smitty could hear the players shuffling in. However, now that he was aware the locker room was broken, the absence of his players talking to each other and laughing was obvious. The silence was deafening.

As confident as Coach Smitty was that what was about to happen was the right path forward, he still had butterflies in his stomach. Just then, there was a knock at his office door. Standing in the doorway was Marcellus.

"Coach Washington said you wanted to see me." Marcellus's voice was cold and emotionless.

"Yes, I do. Please take a seat."

"I'd rather stand, if that's okay, Coach."

"Very well, then. Marcellus, I owe you an apology. What I said today, and how I treated you, was wrong. Full stop. I am so sorry for shutting you down and talking down to you the way I did. I cannot imagine the hurt you must have felt when you heard what Davey said. And then when you tried to have a voice and speak up and call "right," right, and "wrong," wrong—something I have repeatedly encouraged and expected you to do—only to have me shut you down and *cancel you* out in the process. That's two wrongs no person should have to experience, especially not from a teammate and coach."

Marcellus looked straight ahead. The hurt clearly still in his face.

As the person making the amends, Coach Smitty knew that his words had to be authentic and sincere, with zero expectations of his apology being accepted; his job was to own his behavior and apologize for it.

Coach Smitty also knew apologies held a lot of potential for all parties. On one end, they give closure and validation; on the other end, they relieve guilt and shame. When done sincerely, an apology is one of the most vulnerable positions a person can put themselves in because it requires total exposure.

Vulnerability, Coach Smitty knew, was a strength.

"I can't take back the words I said or go back in time and change my actions. If I could, I would, in a heartbeat. But what I can do—what I will do—is use everything in my power to make this situation right." Coach Smitty spent the next few minutes sharing his conversation with Coach Washington, what he learned from it, and what the game plan for the rest of practice that day was.

Through it all, Marcellus presented a stoic demeanor. But inside, Marcellus had to work hard to hear what Coach Smitty was saying. In his head was a chorus of competing voices.

The voice of his pain screamed: "You can't trust this man! He just realized he messed up and now he is trying to save himself!"

The voice of empathy would counter: "He has never treated you like that before. He is human, and humans make mistakes."

The voices of cynicism and revenge would say: "He needs you to win. He is using you. Don't let him win. Hurt him like he hurt you."

There was another voice in Marcellus's head that spoke. It was the most difficult of all to hear, because it didn't shout or push its way to the front of his mind. It was the voice of grace, and it whispered over and over again: "You have the power to forgive. You have the power to heal."

It was finally Coach Smitty's voice that snapped him out of his internal tug-of-war.

"Marcellus? Are you okay?"

"Yes, sir. This is just. . . . This is a lot. I don't know what to say. Thank you for saying something to me in private. It would have looked like a show if you only apologized in front of the team." It was half-hearted, but the best Marcellus could manage.

"You don't owe me a thing, Marcellus. Especially not any gratitude. I owe you that. But know this: I am truly sorry for what I said and did. This is the first step toward me making it right. Let's go talk to the team."

Coach Washington watched as Marcellus and Coach Smitty came out of the office and saw the pained expressions on their faces. He knew apologies and healing never came easy, but then again, why should they? Real hurt requires a real price to be paid, to bring healing.

On the table outside the locker room was a bag of footballs. Coach Smitty grabbed a ball out of the bag, tucked it under his arm, and gave Coach Washington a nod before walking to the center of the locker room. Standing in the silent locker room, directly on their Northwest Tigers logo, Coach Smitty blew his whistle.

12

Team Meeting

"Gentlemen, I need your attention, please," Coach Smitty said to the team, as 72 upset, confused, and wounded young men turned to face him. Many had their arms folded across their chests. It pained Coach Smitty to see his team so dispirited, so disappointed, but the hope of bringing healing, and defeating this opponent called division, urged him forward to action. He swallowed a basketball-sized lump in his throat, and began.

"Everyone, put your pads and helmets in your locker and take a seat. We're not going to the practice field today. Today, we're practicing here, in the locker room."

The players looked around at each other, confused. Coach Smitty continued. "We're not going to physically practice today because our biggest opponent is not out on the field; our biggest opponent is right here."

As Coach Smitty looked around the locker room, intentionally locking eyes with individual players for just a moment, his gaze came to Coach Washington. He could see the pride in his eyes, and the belief that Coach Washington had in him. This gave him courage.

"Men, I owe all of you an apology. As your head coach and leader, I let all of you down. I lowered the standard and there is no excuse for that. I didn't live up to the standard of the Six Pillars with how I handled Davey's situation." Heads turned to Davey, who put his head down, staring at the floor, getting red in the face.

Coach Smitty said to Davey, "Pick that chin up, Davey. You made a big mistake. Your words and actions let this team down and caused real hurt to men who treated you like a brother, a teammate."

Davey slowly raised himself back up.

Coach Smitty continued, "As you all know by now, last Friday night, Davey said some very hurtful, insensitive, and stupid things which were recorded and put out all over social media. When I found out about it, I, and I alone, made the decision to handle the situation privately. In fact, my best friend in the entire world, Coach Washington, urged me to handle it in the open, as a team. Unfortunately, I ignored his advice. I'm sorry, Coach Washington."

Coach Washington, not wanting to interrupt this moment, gave Coach Smitty a thumbs up, high enough for every man to see.

"Do you men know why I ignored Coach Washington's advice?" Coach Smitty asked, rhetorically. "Fear! Fear of what other people would do or say or think. I was afraid for Davey—that his mistake would get him canceled out and ruin his life. I was afraid for our season—that this would be a distraction to our team, and take away our chances to win the state championship this year.

"I feared doing or saying the wrong thing and what that might mean for my own career. But the thing that I am most ashamed of is that I was never afraid of what hurt and pain my actions would cause our players of color. When this hit, I thought about everyone and everything except the ones who were most hurt by Davey's words. I am so very sorry to each of you. I signed the contract the same as each of you, and my failure to live up to our standards led to great hurt. You deserve more respect and dignity than I showed you."

No person in that locker room had ever seen anything like that happen before. The head football coach, canceling practice to . . . apologize? As divided as this team was, they were united in their silence and shock. Then, Coach Smitty turned his attention to Marcellus. "Marcellus, I owe you the biggest apology. As I said in my office, you don't owe me a thing. But I want the team to hear me tell you this. I treated you wrong. And I am truly sorry for that. You are a great athlete, but an even better young man and leader. It's a privilege to be your coach, and I hope you can find it in your heart to forgive me."

Marcellus was fighting back tears through clenched teeth. He was torn between what he felt he wanted and what he knew was right.

After a pause, Coach Smitty said, "We have a broken locker room, gentlemen. Which means Friday night doesn't matter anymore. What matters is that this team, this family, finds a way to heal and become whole. To do that, we are going to turn back to the Six Pillars, and we are going to have to communicate. We are going to have a difficult conversation today about racism and we will not leave this locker room until every man in here feels like he has been heard.

"This conversation is going to require us to be tough. But that's why one of our pillars is TOUGH PEOPLE WIN. We must be tough enough to communicate, and we must be tough enough to show humility and grace. When humility and grace are present, there is no room for racism or division. Today, we are going to learn from one another, and listen to each other. Today, we restore love back into this family."

He held up the football. "This football in my hand is like the microphone. Whoever holds it gets to speak until they have said anything and everything they want to say. If you don't have the ball, you're not allowed to speak. No exceptions. So, who wants the ball first?"

The first hand to go up was Coach Washington's. Coach Smitty nodded and tossed him the ball.

13

Humility and Grace

All eyes were on Coach Washington in the packed and silent locker room. He was proud of his friend for taking charge and being vulnerable. Coach Smitty's passionate and authentic plea was working. The energy had shifted and the team was listening.

Coach Washington wanted the ball first because he knew it was important for the players of color to hear from him immediately. Having been the minority in many rooms, he could empathize with their apprehension to participate in a group forum where everyone would get to speak freely on such a sensitive topic.

Holding the football up high, to show he had the floor, Coach Washington began.

"Thank you for your sincerity and your willingness to admit your mistake, Coach Smitty. That requires humility, a necessary ingredient if we are going to fix our broken locker room.

"Gentlemen, I will always shoot straight with you. Like you, I signed the contract that requires INTEGRITY OVER EVERYTHING. This conversation, in this locker room, is unlike any conversation I have ever been invited to engage in. As a Black man, I have never been asked by a white man, in a room full of people, to share my experiences regarding racism."

His face was stern, but on the inside he was smiling. This was progress. Just like the Six Pillars stated: GROWTH FOLLOWS BELIEF. Coach

Washington believed this was going to be a powerful conversation, where healing, forgiveness, and growth would take place. As a coach, he could not have asked for a more teachable moment. This, he knew, was what coaching these young men was all about. How much closer would this team be today after this practice?

"I wanted this ball first because I want to be heard, just like I know many of you—especially those of you who look like me—want to be heard. I encourage all of you to grab this football today and be heard."

The players' heads were nodding in unison, locked in on Coach Washington. Keeping the momentum of the moment, he continued, telling them about the difficult conversation Coach Smitty and he had, the differences between racism and prejudice, his own experiences with both, and his thoughts about how destructive cancel culture is to resolving racial issues.

Once he felt as though he had been heard, he shared with them the simple—yet, at times, elusive—ingredients necessary to navigate this difficult topic: humility and grace.

"When a person comes to you, wanting to learn and *willing to listen with humility*, then it's your responsibility to respond and *teach that person with grace*," he said, his voice raised at just the right times for effect. "Where humility and grace are present, there is no room for racism, division, or cancel culture—only healing and progress."

Coach Washington saw the players in the room begin to soften their stares and relax their postures. The players were now looking around at each other, as if noticing for the first time they were in a packed locker room. The simple gesture of making eye contact with one another was the indication he was looking for.

Coach Washington continued, "This is a chance for us all to grow, but we must listen with our hearts as well as our minds. For those of you who look like me, I need you to trust your family in this room, show grace, share your thoughts and experiences, and be ready to teach and listen. For those of you who look like Coach Smitty, I'm not asking you to be a punching bag. I'm asking you to listen to your brothers in this room who are of different races, cultures, ethnicities, and backgrounds. I'm also asking you to share your thoughts and experiences because relationships and communication are two-way streets."

As a coach, it was always important to understand when he had coached a lesson to the right point; over-coaching could cause a player to shut down and tune out. Coach Washington felt like he was at that point. He concluded by saying, "One final thought. One of our pillars is EXCELLENCE EVERYWHERE. That is especially important in this conversation. Words are powerful. Once spoken, they can never be unsaid. Choose your words wisely, so that we can all learn from each other. Now, who wants this football?"

Multiple arms shot up. The team was eager to communicate. One by one, the football was passed around. The teammates shared their personal experiences regarding racism and how Davey's comments made them feel.

A Black athlete spoke up and shared a personal experience. "One time my family went to this really nice dinner for my mom's birthday. It was one of those places where everyone was in suits and nice dresses, only I was wearing my hoodie because it was cold outside. From the moment we walked in, it just felt like everyone was looking at us, 'cause we were the only Black people in there. I don't know if they were or not, but I do know that I felt so out of place and uncomfortable. Like I didn't belong there. To be honest, that was the same feeling I had when I heard what Davey said. Like, whoa. Maybe I don't belong on this team. It really hurt."

Next, a white athlete spoke up, "I hate what Davey said, but he is my friend. I've gotten three or four different texts today calling me a racist for still being friends with him. I don't think that he is a racist or that I am. I think he made a mistake. I'm really sorry for the hurt his words caused. I don't know if I am allowed to not give up on my friend, and still call what he said and did wrong? I really hope so. Because I love Davey, and I love my teammates of color. I just want us to be on the same team on and off the field."

For more than two hours the team shared story after story with one another. It was a true example of the team's pillar of RELENTLESS EFFORT—proving their commitment and love for one another by their effort and actions. Some athletes shared that they had never experienced racism or prejudice, and others told heart-wrenching stories of the times their humanity was devalued. Some athletes talked about their families, and others talked about the doubts and questions they had, but none of them ever attacked Davey. They were clear: his actions hurt and didn't meet the team standard, but they never attacked him. As Coach Smitty listened, learned, and took notes, he was in awe of how respectful and open each of these young men was being. The longer the conversation went on, however, the closer the football came to Davey and the elephant in the room: What would he do about Davey?

For his part, Davey sat silently, and listened to each player. After every player had a chance to hold the ball, Davey asked for it so he could speak. When Davey caught the ball, the tension in the room returned, and every set of eyeballs turned toward the star quarterback.

14

I Want the Ball

Davey was known on the football field, and in recruiting circles, for his "poise," that intangible, difficult-to-coach quality that allows a player to remain balanced and calm in the most stressful situations.

Today, however, Davey was anything but poised. His nervousness facing the team was visible, his anxiety high. For the past two hours, he had listened to his teammates and heard how much pain, negativity, and distraction his words had caused. Had he known the power of his words, he would have never said something so insensitive and ignorant.

Ignorant.

That's exactly what he felt like, too. Until today, he had no clue what his words truly meant. Nevertheless, he knew ignorance was no excuse for making poor choices. And, poor choices have consequences.

He held the football tight, mostly out of nervousness. As he scanned the room, he thought about how different the lives of so many of his teammates were from his own. It was as if he lived in a bubble that protected him from so much in the world. Until today, he had never understood what the big deal was regarding the topic of race because he had never stopped to think about things from someone else's perspective.

Davey knew his actions had let everyone down and that he had hurt the people in this room he cared about most. He was not sure he could make it right, but he felt he could certainly try. With all the determination he brought to a two-minute drill, Davey addressed his teammates.

"I'm so sorry, guys. So incredibly sorry. I'm sorry for the hurtful words I said and for the way I handled myself after. I did not practice the character of a leader. I lacked integrity and was selfish.

"Most of us have grown up together from elementary school on. Yet, after listening to each of you today, I realize I have never truly known what most of your lives are like. Which means, on top of being insensitive with the things I said, I have been incredibly self-absorbed."

Everyone was locked in on Davey. The impassive looks on their faces were impossible to read.

"I do not feel as though I deserve the grace you all have shown me today. You each treated me better than I treated you," Davey admitted. "Thank you for teaching me through your grace. It's a lesson I'll never forget. There are no words I can say that will change what I did. Whether I am your quarterback moving forward or not, my actions will show that I have learned my lesson."

Turning to Coach Smitty, Davey said, "Coach, I violated the contract and did not live up to our standard of behavior. I'm sorry. I accept the consequences."

Coach Smitty was about to respond, when he heard someone say, "I want the ball!"

Everyone turned around to see Marcellus, with his hand raised.

After two hours of hearing about his teammates' hurts and experiences, Marcellus no longer had a chorus of voices arguing in his head. All but one voice had been silenced.

"Coach, I don't know if there has ever been anyone who has pushed me harder, or believed in me more than you. I actually believed you when you told me I could make it to the next level. I believed you when you told me you wanted me to be more vocal and lead. I believed you when you told me the Six Pillars would change my life. And then today happened.

"When I did what you told me to do, and held you to the standard of the Six Pillars, you snapped at me. It wasn't about the yelling. I can handle that. It felt like you set me up and used me. It was as if everything you told me to believe in was really just to get me to play better so you could use me to win a championship. I felt like a fool for believing you cared about me."

Turning to Davey, Marcellus said, "Davey, we've been friends since we were in the fifth grade. Or, at least, I thought we were. Even when I saw that video, I thought, 'There is no way Davey would say that!' That was my first thought, Davey! I never thought you would say something so hurtful, ignorant, and racist, because I thought you felt the way about me that I did about you."

Davey started to speak up, but Marcellus held the ball up to stop him.

"I've been called racial slurs before, Davey. So it's not about that. It's about the fact that *you* devalued *me*, and an entire group of your teammates who would do anything for you, all so you could get a laugh at a party. That hurts, Davey.

"All day I've been wrestling with what to do or say. I've been ready to quit; I've been ready to fight; and I've been ready to just scream and cry. I've felt it all." Marcellus started to speak again, but paused to look at his teammates for the first time. "But it wasn't until I heard all of you speak, that I felt ready to *forgive*. Coach Smitty, it hurt how you treated me. Davey, what you said and did was wrong. But if I've learned anything in this locker room, I've learned that making a mistake doesn't make you a mistake. We are all imperfect people and we all come from different backgrounds, with different hurts, hang-ups, and history. But that diversity of life, experiences, and culture isn't something that we have to overcome; it's something we must harness to each become the fullest version of ourselves. We all make mistakes, but we can also all make each other better.

"Everything in me wanted to see you booted off the team, Davey. But the truth of the matter is that in a Locker Room, your success is my success, and my success is yours. *We* are linked! *We* are equal! *We* are stronger together than we will ever be apart.

This isn't about the scoreboard; this is about life. We can use this moment to turn and run from each other in anger, or we can choose to come together, heal this hurt, and overcome this adversity—together. I forgive you, Coach Smitty. I forgive you, Davey. Thank you all for letting me share."

And with that, Marcellus tossed the ball to Coach Smitty and the locker room erupted into cheers and applause! Teammates quietly broke out their game-day chant, first one voice, then another, until a mighty chorus sang with one voice:

"NORTH! WEST! NORTH! WEST! T-I-G-E-R-S TIGERS! TIGERS! We're the BEST!"

As the cheering calmed down, Coach Smitty blew his whistle and held up the football. The team took a knee to listen to their coach. "Thank you, Marcellus. For more than I can say. Thank you."

Marcellus nodded at his coach with a big smile.

"But the standards are the standards," Coach Smitty said. "If we've learned anything from this, it's that we can't lower the standards, for anyone or for any reason. Davey still has to run his punishment miles, and they must be completed before he can compete again."

Marcellus stood up sharply. Coach Smitty nodded approval for him to speak. "I'm sorry to interrupt you, Coach Smitty. But the sixth pillar is SERVICE BEFORE SELF. I can't speak for the team, but I can speak for me, as a team captain. I volunteer to do his punishment miles *with* him, so that he can have them done by Friday."

Whoa! Davey couldn't believe what he was hearing. Why would Marcellus, a victim of his remarks, be willing to do his punishment with him? "Marcellus, I'm humbled by your gesture," Davey jumped up and into the conversation, "but I can't let you do that. Your forgiveness is more than I deserve. This punishment is my responsibility and I owe it to you guys."

Another player stood up, and said, "I'll run with him, too." Before Davey could protest, every member of the team was standing, ready to run Davey's miles with him.

Then Davey, through tears of gratitude, said, "I don't know what to say. Thank you all so much. I'll never let you down again."

"We know you won't, Davey." Marcellus encouraged. "It's like Coach Washington said, 'When humility and grace are present, there is only room for healing and progress.'"

Then, to the team Marcellus said, "Okay, Tigers! We got some miles to run to get our boy Davey back right with the contract. Let's break it out and lace 'em up! Northwest on three! One . . . two . . . three . . . NORTHWEST!

Epilogue: A Legacy of Impact: The Lifetime Achievement Award Acceptance Speech

Like many coaches, Coach Smitty was a gifted speaker who knew how to tell a story. He made everyone in the room feel like he was talking directly to them, even in this room with hundreds of people. No one moved the entire time he spoke. Even the waiters and waitresses stopped what they were doing to listen to his story.

"After that locker room meeting, men were hugging each other as if we had won a championship. And, in a way, we had won a championship. Coaches, players, everyone," Coach Smitty said, as he gazed out into the room from the podium.

Wiping away tears, Coach Smitty admitted, "I know this will probably come as a surprise to everyone here, but I was crying like a baby after Marcellus spoke."

Laughter could be heard throughout the crowd, as Coach Smitty was known for being *extremely* transparent with his emotions.

Coach Smitty told the crowd that the first person he hugged was his best friend, Coach Washington.

"I held him close and told him how much I loved him, and how grateful I was for his friendship. With humility and grace, we were able to repair our broken locker room and bring our team closer together than ever before."

He continued, telling the crowd that they went on to win that Friday night and, eventually, winning out to take home the state championship trophy after an undefeated season. "In our field house, there is a mural painted on the wall of the iconic picture of Marcellus and Davey, on the shoulders of their teammates, hoisting up the trophy together."

The crowd gasped, as the screen behind Coach Smitty lit up with the picture of Marcellus and Davey. In true Coach Smitty fashion, he elicited every ounce of emotion from his audience to drive his point home.

He wasn't finished, either.

"The difficult conversation in the locker room that day was the beginning of a friendship that has seen Marcellus and Davey be best men at each other's weddings and godfathers to each other's children," he said, pointing to the screen behind him.

"What happened in the locker room that day was a transformation of hearts and minds, lasting beyond that football season. A legacy of making an impact was created when these two men founded a nonprofit that works to create equality and address the imbalance of power that is racism. Together, their impact is felt by children of color all over our great country." Coach Smitty paused, ramping up to his grand finale.

"Now, imagine if all Americans used that same prescription of humility and grace to not only resolve issues of racism but all differences. I tell you: America needs a Locker Room!

"In a Locker Room, when you make a mistake, it doesn't make you a mistake. There are consequences for our mistakes, but healthy Locker Rooms use those consequences to restore, not cancel."

Raising his voice for effect, Coach Smitty exclaimed, "In a healthy Locker Room, your success is my success, and my success is yours. *We* are linked! *We* are equal! *We* are stronger together than we will ever be apart."

Gripping the sides of the podium tightly, Coach Smitty leaned into the microphone, slowly scanned the crowd, and spoke his truth. "I love America, and I know you do, too. It's the greatest country in the world. But the coach in me says that, no matter how great you are, there's always room for improvement. Room to be better. Room to grow. And, growth takes place outside your comfort zone."

Beaming at the crowd with his trademark smile, Coach Smitty concluded, "I have faith, and truly believe we will get there together. And make no mistake, sports will lead the way. It always has. One day, America will have her Locker Room.

"God bless, you all, and God bless America!"

The room erupted in applause as Coach James "Smitty" Smith waved goodbye one final time to a cheering crowd. As he exited the stage, Coach Washington, Marcellus, and Davey were waiting for him with tears in their eyes—for they all knew that this speech, and the message within it, would go down as Coach Smitty's greatest victory.